Silver Pen
Psalms & Prayers

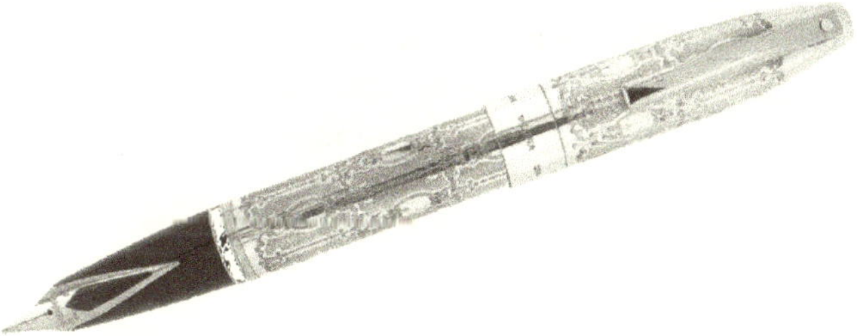

ROBERT SIMMS

SILVER PEN PSALMS AND PRAYERS
by Robert F. Simms

Published by Robert F. Simms
204 Sheffield Rd, Greer, South Carolina 29651

ISBN: 978-1-7378117-6-3
Printed in the United States of America

1

Lord, you have defied the fullest praise,
for your acts are unknown to us in full.
Yet praise is due you to the fullest,
to the limit of our limited minds.
We struggle to glorify you with our lips
because we know our limitations.
Yet we do not know them, in truth,
because we do not know ourselves;
We see ourselves as a beast might see,
and do not comprehend the depths.
Therefore, how can we see you in full,
in your glory, and praise you well?
But our lips will speak your praise,
weakly but from a plaintive heart.
And your ear will hear it well,
and you will accept it as good.

2

O Lord, I am brought low
by the infirmities that have come upon me.
They have sought me out;
they have put their target on me,
That they might increase my sorrows
and multiply my woes.
But they are not able to overcome you,
who well up in my soul.
My joy defiant, and my faith victorious,
when day after day I must rise up.
I call to you, my God, to strengthen me,
to make me stand when I am bowed low.
I call to you, my Lord, who bore my sins,
to bear my burden now,
For it is too much for me,
and I am plowed under by its weight.

3

Surely, my God, my praise must come,
    a discipline of a fervent heart,
The product of determined devotion,
    even in a dry land and a time of want.
Not into the void do I speak my words,
    though often on a dark morning they
Seem to ring hollow, or disappear into
    the void of heaven's spacious maw.
For my deafness to your voice is not evidence
    of your unwillingness to speak,
But a sign of my failure to hear,
    the product of the dullness of my inner ear.
Until I am attuned to your voice, Lord,
    I will speak your praise and
I will seek your face, and you will
    speak, and I will say, "I hear."

4

Oh, in the worship of my heart, Lord,
    you spoke to me, within my soul!
On the heights of praise your people sang,
    lifting up your holiness,
And my heart was broken again,
    my spirit set free from the daily shackles,
The trouble of this earth that plagued me,
    and with the saints I gloried in you.
Pierce my life with the wonder of your being,
    and let me but glimpse your glory.
Keep me, then, in humble worship,
    my soul in Christ attuned to you.
Refresh my spirit with your moving,
    your inexplicable moving,
And keep me close to you, where angels sing,
    and where saints lose themselves in holiness.

5

My heart is moved, my memory stirred,
when I think on days with friends,
Who with me sought to follow after you,
O Lord my Savior and my God.
In your presence they now exult in praise,
while I yearn from here, alone.
O Father of all glory, Son of Creation Power,
by your Spirit reach into my heart,
Comfort and sustain me here,
until I walk ashore to your abode.
Light my path, my Guide,
steady my walk in you.
As my steps grow weak from years,
may my travel be sure-footed at heart,
And fit me for everlasting life, which
you have long ago given to my soul.

6

From the rough land of painful trudging
    I come into a brief, pleasant place,
And am relieved, though before me lies
    a thicket of wearisome travel.
I am thankful, my Lord, for this relief,
    and I am confused by the prospect before me.
How long, my God, will I be tried?
    How long will you lead me through pain?
What purpose is in your mind for me,
    and what end does your wisdom intend?
I see only trial, and my heart is weary.
    I cannot see light before me except
What lies in eternity, where you are,
    beyond the veil of death.
I long to be in your presence, O Christ,
    to be free from this pathway of tears.

7

Holy God, apart from all yet filling all,
I share with all on earth in this, that
We have but lately known in all history
that your creation is so utterly vast,
And we are even more the specks of dust
the ancients knew we were,
And in a corner of this vast expanse
more than we ever knew.
How then can we dream that you care
what transpires in our isolated lives,
When for all we know you tend millions
of populations throughout myriad galaxies
And hear the cacophony of their pleas
and cries and the appeals of their worship?
Except that you have said you do care, and we
believe it, for you are God, Omniscient.

8

I gave way to the sin that first enslaves all men,
in those early years when my will asserted itself.
I gave to the convicting Spirit my heart in repentance
when he showed me the dark death ahead.
I gave in to the Lordship and will of Jesus Christ
when he held out his saving hand to mine.
I gave over my life to his perfect calling
when he bade me serve in his kingdom.
I gave to his kingdom cause all I could, though
human frailty sometimes marred my deeds.
I gave out of courage at times of great stress,
and I prayed to recover to go on to serve.
I gave through my deep trial all I could to God,
and he supplied my need with his plenty.
If I give up on the hope of his purpose now,
I shall miss what God wants to do yet.

9

Help me, O my Lord, help me!
I cry at daybreak and all day long.
And I ask your pardon for my complaint,
since I know I should care more for others,
And care more for your glory
and for your kingdom,
And I should pray with praise, and
I should worship you.
Would my paltry concerns be subsumed
in the light of your glory inside me
If I could revel more in who you are
and less in what has plagued me?
Yet daily I hold before you others who hurt,
and those I have committed to ask you to save;
Lord, please bless them, even if you will not
bless me today! I thank you, O my Lord.

10

The king and his singers after him
harked back to days not in their own memory,
Written down for all the tribes who would come,
praising you, O God, for your deliverance.
And we, my Savior and God, have adopted as ours the
history of your people, though grafted into them.
And so this praise I join from my heart of hearts,
thankful to have been foreseen as a son.
But to these ancient memories I add, O Lord,
the recounting of my own.
For you have been my rock, my guide and
my deliverer oft through them you gave me,
Who were my father and my mother,
who like those before them knew you.
In somber yet joyous faith I remember them,
and thank you, Heavenly Father, for them.

11

In a dark place of trouble and pain
I glimpse the light of your presence, Lord.
It pierces my night, the cracked door of heaven,
your glory beyond, awaiting me.
Oh how long will it be, my Savior,
Until I escape this struggle, either here,
Or hereafter? How long until I am relieved,
for a while, or forever with you?
I call out to you. I trust you. You know me;
you know how long I can prevail here.
Send more light, Lord! Let it flood this place.
Let it engulf me, reveal me, guide me.
And speak to me, through the angel's song,
or through the silent voice of my better mind,
And tell me again of your love, that
cannot be diminished. Yea, Lord! Amen.

12

From my deeper soul, my Lord and Friend,
I give up to you the quiet praise you deserve.
For though my flesh aches and woes increase,
I cannot withhold your due, my worship of you.
Others this day may be able to render happy praise,
the ready worship of those with lives in sunshine.
As for me, my internal joy must be enough,
my inner peace for knowing my salvation,
My inward strength, withstanding outward pain,
giving rise to worship, obligatory but not coerced.
I say, "Praise God." I say, "I worship you."
And no falsity is in my mouth or heart.
And I hope that when they who lift their hands,
in happiness to sing your name,
Have entered times of trouble, they may render
worship still, knowing you are God, either way.

13

You command the armies of the world, Lord.
They do your bidding, unknown to themselves.
And to their peril they attack at will,
though you sovereignly ordain it.
How can it be other, God? When you are God?
Can any thwart you or evade you?
So the unseen enemy plagues me time to time,
as if he—it—is in command.
And so did the accuser plague Job of old,
but he was permitted, for you are in charge.
It is too deep for me, though I know it deeply.
It is too high for me; yet I am sure of it.
And so I surrender my plagued body
to your sovereign will, knowing your goodness.
And I plead your mercy, that I may live
in peace, and health, and sing your praise.

14

I will not forget your blessings in my life,
O my Great Provider, and Giver of every good gift.
I remember my oft idyllic youth, safe from harm,
nestled in a loving family and secure home.
I recall your presence felt in the hearts and hands
of those who reared me and guided me.
I remember your provision during hard years
when uprooted and planted in another place.
I am mindful of your hand upon me to live for you,
to give a testimony with my word and life.
I know you put a hedge around me,
when days of foolishness tempted me.
I recall the companionship of brotherly love,
and the clarity of your call to me.
And I thank you, my Redeemer and Friend,
for it all, and pray I shall never forget.

15

Do you speak to me, you Orator of Creation?
Have you spoken to me in the night time?
And have I failed to hear you, or have I
mistaken your words for sounds in a dream?
Have you spoken in broad daylight, and have I
taken your words for my own thoughts?
Have you spoken in my imagination, or have I
merely imagined that you spoke?
How can I know your voice, you Speaker of Heaven,
if I cannot say where the cacophony ends?
How can I hear you above my own mind's voice,
and know what you have to say?
Your word is ancient and yet new,
your voice eternal, but speaking now.
Let me hear you, that I might be led,
and that I might know you more.

16

Into the sanctuary of my own heart and mind
  I come, Father, to open my heart in silent praise.
Into the temple of my soul where you dwell
  I come, Holy Spirit, to bare that soul in worship.
Into your inexpressible presence in my life
  I come, Divine Son and Redeemer, to offer thanks.
I am wordless before you, yet full of words
  that cannot be spoken.
If by your own being in me you groan
  and do not utter it,
Who am I to think I can orate before you
  and fully speak my case?
As the singer before me, I stand in awe,
  vowing only to sin not, and I am still.
Yet stir up the eternal song in me, O God,
  that my life might be a psalm to you.

17

The King of Creation listens to me.
He pays attention to my prayer.
They who lampoon the truth that God is infinite
and they who do not believe the Almighty cares
Are together in folly and unaware of how foolish,
how altogether ignorant they are.
Their small god, who cannot do all things,
who is not in every place all the time
Is altogether unworthy to be called god,
and they have conceived him in rebellion.
My God surrounds me and inhabits me;
he knows me to the deepest depth.
He has let me see a little of his light
and it draws me into his presence.
But I hunger for more light, that I may know you,
and see you forever in your glorious presence.

18

What am I in this vast creation, my God?
Who am I among all you have made?
What importance has my brief existence had,
among all who have lived?
What have I done, O Lord Almighty,
whose plan is vast and sweeping?
You called me unto yourself in your time;
you set me in a place to live and serve.
I thought my life meant something
to others, to your kingdom, in this time.
I cannot see it now, Lord, as I look at it.
I cannot measure it, against any rule.
You alone, Sovereign God, know what I am,
and you alone know why you put me here.
I shall wait on the revelation of eternity to see it.
I then shall nod in peace and final joy.

19

I love you, Lord. I do. I try to love you,
with my whole heart and in my ways.
But who can know his heart?
It is dark in places, in depths unplumbed.
Can I know what I love that is not of you?
Can I even tell if I have reserved some part?
I tell my own heart that I love you.
I speak to it what I know you want.
Soften my heart to you, Lord;
make me vulnerable to your Spirit.
Fill my heart with wonder of you,
with awe of you, with praise of you.
Displace my dispassion with free worship,
and my reserve with enthusiasm for you.
Then shall I, as David, sing a new song,
and those who hear will be drawn to you.

20

I think upon your infinity, God,
that you are infinitely everything good.
And I realize that if condescending to things
lower than yourself is good,
Then you do not withhold yourself from me,
or from any of your creatures.
For while man may believe he alone is
created in the image of God specially,
You put something of yourself in everything;
your beauty in me—or in all,
Your ingenuity in this one or that,
your grace and majesty in others.
And somehow they know you—not as we do,
but they know they are yours.
And they, too, yearn incomprehensibly for
the day all creation shall be set right.

21

If you had not shown yourself, Infinite One,
we had not known you at all.
But like a divine parade, you showed yourself,
bit by bit, that we might take it in.
The glittering heavens sparkled out front,
drawing childlike eyes, with fascination.
The pageantry of their dance in the skies,
their marching through our day and night.
Then you laid out the intricate ranks of life,
the diminutive spokesmen of the divine creator.
A voice rang out, to chosen marchers,
the plan of your holy procession revealing.
Marvels performed in the streets of your coming:
the One about whom the spectacle was created.
And soon he will come in all his glory, the end
of the parade, but the beginning of Infinite Glory!

22

Your servant Moses heard you speak, knew you,
and still asked that you show yourself to him.
Your son David waxed eloquent in praise
and halted to plead, When will you come to me?
Your disciple Thomas you graciously accommodated
with your hands and feet to convince.
And even John, greater than whom was no prophet,
you gently convinced with your words.
I am no greater than any before me,
indeed, not equal to any of these,
And I ask no more than they,
indeed, even less, that you move in me,
That you encounter me that I may you,
that I may know you more.
To that end I thank you and praise you,
Ever Living One, my Gracious God.

23

O for the still, small voice
    the prophet heard in his mountain.
To hear, though after a tempest dulls my ear,
    the certain though quiet whisper of God.
To know, though senses otherwise deny it,
    the words of the Spirit of the Almighty!
O Lord God, shouter of your name in creation,
    speaker of your wisdom in design,
You teacher of your truths in history,
    and whisperer of your love,
You proclaimer of mercy in salvation's gospel,
    whose wind filled rooms and hearts,
Blow mightily into my soul and whisper there
    the loving intent of your presence.
And make me to know the fullness of your person
    in the small voice I hear only deep within.

24

At midnight I wake and sleep then escapes me.
    Have you come to me in the darkness?
I think of you and I turn my spirit to you,
    to worship in ignorance of your purpose.
Do you want me to cry to you, to plead a cause?
    To lift up a name?
Do you want me to listen only, silent of heart,
    awaiting revelation or an answer?
I seize upon every thought as cause to pray,
    and I listen for any voice not mine.
Content that you are in control
    I thank you for the gift of sleep again.
I praise you that I do not awake troubled,
    out of guilt or fear,
But that when I wake, I know you are near,
    for you protect me and give me true rest.

25

The little animals around me trust me,
seek me out, for no need except to be.
They depend upon me, having surrendered
their lone hunting to my generous hand.
And when sleep comes upon them they
delight to repose with me.
O Sovereign and Infinite God of all creation,
you have sewn into our being a thread,
A trace, a pattern, a color of yourself,
that we might come to you and relate to you.
And diminutive as we are compared to you,
we should trust you, and seek you.
For though we may eke out a living
while ignorant of your benevolence,
How much greater joy to receive from your hand
and rest in your eternal arms, content to be!

26

Against the deep night sky, O Creator,
    your swath of uncountable stars
Stretches out in purple hues, dotted bright,
    an arm's reach and an infinite stretch away.
Oh how small I am, Mighty One, how small,
    lost in the universe but for this:
You know me, know my mind, know my heart,
    and you have chosen me,
To be one of your people, each of whom
    you know as you know me,
And each one of whom you love,
    as you love me—inexplicably.
I wonder at our place in this vast space.
    I wonder at your purpose.
And I praise and worship you in it,
    that I might find it and do it, for your glory.

27

The vision of your everlasting throne, O God,
in the place where the apostle saw
The light of the Glorious Lord would be our day
and never night should darken it,
I see now was the picture of your formal abode,
where your presence is displayed,
And where exalted beings ever praise you,
and where saints of the ages will worship.
But out in the galaxies made new
we shall live and explore in peace and joy,
And revel quietly in the glorious nights,
your stars displaying your infinite might.
And on this sweet and quiet night,
while creatures sing and chirp in praise,
I, too, surrender my silent worship to you,
O God of sacred darkness and holy light.

28

The rain of life's disciplines, under your rule, Lord,
has softened the ground of my daily life.
The seeds that only you know how long have lain there
have been washed over by daily life.
And now, they sprout, tentatively, but green,
and I know not what these new things may bring.
Will I bear fruit in my increasing years?
Shall someone yet be fed by fruit you produce in me?
I cannot, I must not forfeit my future
for the barrenness of relaxation only.
Temptation prods me toward easy rest.
But your Spirit is restless in me.
You urge me on—to what, my Holy Leader?
Shall an old man run? Perform a mission?
If you will it, Divine Commander, I will do your
bidding, be it to run or to stay.

29

Glory to God, who reigns over all the Universe!
    Glory to him who directs men and nations.
Glory to the One who is sovereign over all,
    be they doers of evil or good,
For evil men and nations shall come to their ends,
    and receive justice for their rebellion.
The Lord has made them vessels for his purposes,
    for how could it be otherwise?
I do not ask, O Lord, that you explain
    how your plan for this world works,
Or even that you show me how your plan
    for my small life has been purposed.
For though I crave at times to know why
    I have gone through trials and valleys,
I thank you for showing me to ask, not why,
    but what now I should do to obey you. Amen.

30

Out under cloudy skies in your lovely heavens
    I ride, escaping the tedium behind,
And I revel in your creation's beauty,
    O God of creation's magnificence.
The mountains in the distance are your stairs
    to the clouds, and the clouds your veil of heaven.
We have come to understand what natural causes
    make our world go around,
But you created the causes, and the elements,
    and without you there was nothing.
Before the rain falls I return, and I know
    that without your plan, I have none.
Without your life, I have no life,
    and without you, I am nothing.
Thank you, Sovereign Lord, that you made me,
    and chose me to discover you. I praise you, Lord!

31

Let every day be the day of worship, Lord!
        Let every day be perfect for praise!
Let every waking of mine be to drink in your grace
    and speak out your goodness to me!
So easily, my Master, do I succumb to temptation
    to complain of all that plagues me.
Though you have said to bring my cares to you,
    help me to cry out between words of thanks.
For you have been inexplicably good to me—
    except that your goodness is who you are.
So when the night of rest is done and
    I must face another day,
Weak and weary and beset with trouble,
    let me remember instead that
You are wonderfully good, and you save me,
    for now, and for eternity soon to come!

32

I am alone, my God, alone in my grief.
No one feels my feelings.
Though hands touch my shoulder,
though words of sympathy are spoken,
I am alone, unto myself with my pain,
for no one can share it.
It is not theirs, Omniscient God, only mine;
but you know, for you know me.
But no one I see can see my discomfort;
no one I can touch can touch my loneliness.
And no one can come alongside me inside me
but you, Holy Spirit, my Lord.
And I have gone many days without you—
without the sense of you, the proof of you.
Shall I spend my final years without your touch,
in suspense for the surprise of eternity?

33

I need some good news, God of goodness.
    This is the hour of great need.
I have heard the quiet word of sickness;
    I have heard the urgent voice of warning.
I have answered the somber message,
    sat sobered by the calm pronouncement.
I have staved off trembling because
    I know you and trust you.
I have steered to the star of your plan
    and believed your plan is other.
My Rock, I do not doubt my faith
    or disbelieve my confidence.
But now is the hour for silent suffering
    to be interrupted with heaven's voice.
I need your gospel of goodness
    that I might be whole again.

34

You have taught us, Lord, to pray
    that your kingdom might come.
And daily I do so pray, sometimes urgently.
    But how will my prayer hasten your rule?
How will the prayers of millions who know you
    and are urgent for your kingdom to come
Hasten your defeat of all of earth's evil powers
    and bring the day of your perfect will—
If, Sovereign King, you have set the day,
    known to you but still a mystery to us?
If, as you said, O Christ, to your disciples,
    no one knows the day—not the angels,
Nor any on earth, but only you, O God,
    what can my prayer do?—
Except to urge me on to do your will on earth
    as every being does in heaven?

35

My spirit ascends through the clouds
    and joins the chorus of heaven,
The holy angels who always do your bidding
    and always sing your praises.
I hear their unearthly blend of voices
    like an unknown orchestra in space,
And as they join with each other
    they join with me, reverberating.
My tune they follow and enhance,
    echoing my worship and offering theirs;
Entering into the brightness of your throne
    they hush and we all adore.
You are beyond my description, O Lord,
    beyond even my conception.
I worship you inside myself, where my soul
    becomes one with your awesome Holy Self.

36

Sometimes I stand before you, God,
speechless, because I am dull of spirit.
I have come out of duty, guilty of heart.
I have no words because my heart is blank.
Sometimes I come before you, God,
speechless, out of confusion and frustration;
I have nothing to say because what I feel
is beyond expression yet, muddled in the mind.
Oh, let me come and stand before you, Lord,
speechless because you are glorious
And I cannot find words to express joy
and to communicate my worship!
Let me come with pure heart and mind,
baffled by the beauty of your being.
And in the light of your holiness and power
let me find cleansing, and fullness, and rest.

37

In a perfect earth, Triune God, I praise you
and I worship you with a perfect heart.
I sing to you with perfect emotion as
the angels in heaven do.
I conceive perfect thoughts about your glory
and I speak them in worship of you.
I am deeply aware this hour of my imperfection,
and I am shameful to feel so little.
My heart is not half yours; it is all yours,
but its feelings are dulled and faded.
And yet something in me calls me to worship,
and I strain to join the procession of souls
Into your presence, to render our due,
the praise of your glory, the honor of you.
Help me to sing from my troubled soul,
and to pray from my flickering light.

38

In the generations behind me, Father,
I see my fathers and their sons
And I glory in the heritage they left
for me in my brief pilgrimage here.
I see in my sons what they will leave
to others yet to come, their lives brief, too.
And I pray for them, Eternal God, this day
that they will walk with you.
Let them not be discouraged by dark days,
by dim vision of the path, by defeats;
Let them grasp the truth passed down
from my fathers many before,
And through me, least of them all,
but striving to be faithful to the faith.
And may they, too, hand down faith, that
our whole family may one day abide with you.

39

One man's blood to another man's veins,
a sacrifice, a gift, a blessing.
Who was the nameless man or woman
who sent the liquid of his life, her body,
To sustain the man now lying there,
the dark red sustenance flowing in?
And how thankful he is that someone cared,
though it could be said that the gift,
Precious as it is, will be replaced,
in God's magnificent design.
And as the man watches the crimson flow
enter his own, injured body,
Bringing life for a little while yet,
he closes his eyes in prayer:
Thank you, Divine Donor, for this small gift,
and for the eternal gift of the blood of the Son.

40

From time immemorial the waves have come,
pounding upon the sand, restrained.
You have said you set their boundaries,
yet they pound in protest.
Against my life, My Protector,
adversities beat ceaselessly to destroy.
And they wear away my dross, tireless,
but you have said, Thus far and no more.
I tire of the violence of the enemy.
I am weary of his pounding at my soul.
I turn to you in this hour and I pray.
I yearn for the perfection of my true home.
When will the enmity of these seas of trouble
become calm, and end, a glassy sea?
Your time for me will come, and till then
I wait, expectant, hopeful, assured.

41

I praise you, Lord: may your kingdom come!
May all wrongdoing cease and right prevail!
What may I do in your kingdom, O King?
What will of yours may be mine today?
Leave me not beside myself, hungering,
thirsting for my role in your divine story.
Take me from the sidelines and send me out;
use me in some quest, if only small.
Years gone by I prayed to you, my Lord,
for a task not so great as to defeat me;
I asked for a role not so small
that it would shame me, or your calling.
And now, time dwindling away from me,
I seek one task more, but be with me,
And I will move in your power, to perform.
And then I can rest, and glory in your name.

42

Giver divine, who has given to all,
    and every gift good, though all unworthy:
You give to givers, that they may bless,
    and all to whom they give, to bless you.
Without shame I ask of you, Great Giver,
    the gift of health with which to bless you,
To bless others and therefore imitate you,
    and to return thanks for your love.
O Lord, I would not beg for this gift
    if in giving it you were to burden me,
To relent only to tie some terrible cost
    to the generosity of your healing hand.
And I find no word of yours that says
    that your gifts are laced with discipline or pain.
My arms, therefore, are open: heal me!
    My thanks and praise will rise continually!

43

Lord, they who look up and see nothing
are blind inside, not outside.
And they who listen but hear nothing
have no ears in their dead souls.
I look up and I see what they see,
but I see you upon and within it all.
I tune my ear and I hear you, not out loud,
but in the still, small voice, like Elijah.
For the silence of heaven may be profound,
as when the heavens are as brass:
Every prayer reflected, unanswered,
every plea ignored.
Or to the wicked, no revelation, because
they seek not to believe, but to reject.
But to me today your silence is an answer,
that I may by faith see all, and hear well.

44

The psalmist said the fool has said
in his heart, There is no god.
These fools think themselves wise,
and speak not only in their hearts,
But boldly dare to declare from pulpits of unbelief
that no god lives, that you, O God, live not.
They seek to stop the mouths of the simple;
they say, Who made God?
And they smirk, and their friends with them.
And the darkness surrounds them like a cloud.
O God, Infinite One, Maker of All, Holy Deity,
their god, if they conceive one, is too small.
I plumb the depths of my paltry experience
and find I cannot touch the bottom,
For you are beyond knowing fully, and you will
soon destroy the fool and save the believer.

45

Freely my heart sings your praise, O God,
though the word commands it, and I comply;
Though I am taught to praise, and I conform;
though I am led to praise, and I follow.
Out of the deeps of my heart I praise you;
You have shown yourself God eternal.
How could I ignore who you are, my Creator?
How could I deny your works?
The people of the world walk along, ignorant,
no contemplation of you, Mighty God.
The deceived conceive of a lesser spirit,
unjust in its dealings, or vindictive only.
And your avowed enemies declare war,
hoping to dissuade the lost.
But I praise you, Omnipotent Savior,
and I pray your kingdom will come swiftly.

46

Mover of men's hearts, changer of lives,
I look at many things and pray for change.
I plead with you to sweep over their lives
and show them their weaknesses.
I struggle against their wrong actions,
judging their intentions by their deeds.
They adapt to the world and justify it—
time marches on, they say.
And in the quiet hour, the spotlight on me,
I know that I must confess my own sin.
For they are not guiltless of corruption,
but I am not innocent of stubbornness.
Show me my rebellion, Divine Conqueror.
Light my dark corners and reveal me.
Grant me the grace of repentance, Holy Spirit,
and renew my unity with your true followers.

47

O the joy of friends in the Lord,
who uphold each other from your holy word!
Thank the Lord, everyone who names his name,
for kindred hearts in service to Christ!
Praise the Lord, all you who know him,
for his fellowship and community with us!
Worship the Lord of the true church,
those who are one in him, who is Lord of all!
In our quiet hours we hold each other up,
their faces in our minds before the throne.
We pledge each to the other our prayers,
and invest our time and care in them.
Meet their needs, Omnipotent Helper!
Make them whole in the name of Jesus.
And in your grace toward them, remember us,
and spread your mercy upon us, as well.

48

Is it only through my hardship, Holy Spirit,
that I can learn your power to sustain?
Is it only by deprivation that I learn
the depths of your plenty?
But I will not invite trial that I may learn,
nor welcome testing as if a friend.
If I say, It is more than I can endure,
I am made an ignorant man.
When troubles increase, and I turn to you,
more dependent and earnest than before,
Show me the bright hosts of heaven,
gathered in numberless array
To worship you and to be infused
with your holiness and power.
O Lover of My Spirit, wash me and renew me,
and I shall trade trouble for glory.

49

I am silent before you, Awesome King,
silent and still, as all earth will be.
The time for loud praise exists
and the occasion for exultation,
But this moment, I am silent,
for you have stood and all before you
Honor you, unable to express themselves,
Incapable of enough recognition of you.
Let no thoughts of anything else come;
let not idle thoughts intercede.
Let no wandering ideas creep in,
or distractions interfere.
Let every thought be of your glory,
every idea come from your mind.
And in the pure revery of this moment
let me become gloriously one with you.

50

The vistas before me seem desolate, Lord.
They are barren. They lead nowhere.
My future is bleak, if judged by my view;
what I see is desolate and without happiness.
I know my joy is inward and is secure,
but what I feel is so void of celebration.
You taught us to abide in you
and you would abide in us.
Yet, the visible knowing the invisible,
the touchable experiencing the spiritual,
Sometimes is beyond my ability,
and evades my sincere desire.
I read and I hear an echo of your voice;
I pray and I strain to detect you, speaking.
How much longer will I be in the body
before I shed it to be with you fully?

51

My comrades are in danger, my God!
    They are in dire straits, Lord of Hosts!
I have covenanted with them to pray,
    to lift them up to you, Mighty One,
That you may consider their plights
    and bring your forces against their enemies.
The emissaries of evil have targeted them;
    the ambassadors of the tempter.
They are lost and unable to seek home,
    for some are blind and others deaf.
Save them, Crucified and Risen Savior!
    Deliver them from death, Ever Living One!
And those who know you but suffer disease,
    Heal them, Great Physician.
And as you pass by on your way,
    remember me, too, in your great mercy.

52

Remind me, Ever Present Spirit,
    when I am going through trouble,
When I am going through trial,
    to keep going.
For what will trial benefit me,
    if I give up and cease faithfulness?
And how will trouble work to my gain, if
    when I am exhausted, I lose heart?
Bring alongside me yourself and your words,
    spoken by men of old, inspired.
Bring to mind the struggles of others
    who stood the test and received reward.
Let the multitudes of those who came before
    be like the myriad stars flung against the night,
Lighting my way to victory in the end.
    I praise you now for that certain future!

53

Nearer, Lord. Let me find the niche,
to be nearer to you in this time.
Purer, Lord. Let me be renewed in purity,
and live in greater holiness than before.
Greater, Lord—greater in faith, let me grow.
I cannot now live by sight in dark times.
Bolder, Lord, may I grow in witness,
my life counting for something beyond me.
More tender, Lord; let me sense needs,
and, living out the life of Jesus, touch others.
More loving, Lord. For when all is done,
only love remains.
More hopeful, Lord. Change despair;
make it hope instead, in the light of truth.
More Christlike, Lord. For I shall be fulfilled
when he is all to me, and I am all his.

54

O God untouchable, unseen, unlimited,
    take me beyond this veil of flesh;
Show me your glory, Awesome One,
    and let me be lost in your Eternal Self.
Man conceives of you, for you have created.
    Man senses you, for you have designed.
Some men hear from you in the night,
    for you spoke to them, in rare speech.
Moses pled with you to show yourself,
    and you passed by, a safe glimpse.
I do not ask for revelations to exalt me;
    I do not ask to be apart from others.
I only ask you to help me realize you,
    the God of my prayers, Lord of my heart,
So I may feel your presence, beside Jesus,
    and follow with assurance all my days.

55

O Omnipotent Sufficiency and Grace,
    it should be enough to rest in that.
I should myself be satisfied with your presence,
    which though I may not feel, I know of.
Nothing remotely disproves that you are here,
    all around me, pervasive and omniscient.
And that should be enough for me;
    I could enter prayer, bask in your presence;
I could go on my way, faithful in my day.
    I could say I had prayed, and be done.
But you have told me to make my requests
    known to you, Divine Giver of Love.
And I have poured out to you my heart,
    not for paltry things, but vital things.
And you have not answered me, My God.
    When will you tell me yes, or no?

56

As the gloom and darkness of a stormy day
    give way to the brightness of sunshine,
So a time of worrisome trouble
    yields its threats to your deliverance!
O Powerful Rescuer, I give thanks for your hope
    and praise for your precious promises.
Who can guess your intricate plans
    or know your omniscient resources?
And who can prevent your movements
    or prevail against you in your purposes?
You have ordained that we who follow you
    should walk by faith, not by sight.
We have prayed you would increase that faith
    that we might see inside our souls.
Let us not miss the training of our faith
    by searching with the wrong eyes.

57

I praise you, Worthy God, though
    I don't really know how to praise.
I say words. I sing songs. I play music.
    But I do not yet know how the angels praise.
Shall I merely repeat the scriptures, Lord?
    Have I not some original thought?
Is it enough for me to sing the words of others,
    or repeat the prayers of praise when led?
And if I could compose a psalm of praise
    that uttered every thought I ever had,
That expressed as lofty worship as I am able,
    would that suffice to praise you fully?
Or do you want me to be still before you,
    to come to an utter halt before your majesty,
And open every part of me to you, surrendered,
    in wordless, astounded offering of who I am?

58

Know my thoughts, Omniscient Deity,
  for you do, and perfectly.
When I was a child I was, as all children, self-centered,
  shamelessly, innocently self-absorbed.
I could not know my father's concern for me;
  I did not even guess my mother's worries.
When I became a father, I learned my want.
  And yet, I did not know even then,
I could not feel what now I feel,
  as I see my sons live before you,
Trying to discern your will and do it,
  facing still their futures, hoping for fulfilment.
O Gracious God, where once I saw only my own needs,
  now I am helpless, wanting to guide and bless them.
Be their light, Lord! Be their rock!
  For I am almost gone, and you are their All.

59

Merciful God, though you have unleashed
upon a rebellious world many deserved ills,
And by them have declared the wages of sin,
and through them sometimes turned hearts,
Yet now look upon my friend, whose life is yours,
whose service was yours from his youth.
Who now lies entrapped by evil disease,
which no man's healing can assuage.
Good Savior, what more can his suffering,
which is great, do for your kingdom?
Reach from heaven into our weary world;
take him into your presence!
Let not his precious wife be tortured more,
or his friends stand by, helpless.
Reward your servant with release from bondage;
silently, I will thank you, while still we mourn.

60

O Perfect One in all your attributes,
    you deserve the worship you command.
We are repulsed by dishonorable men
    who expect our honor: they are proud.
Less, we can honor those who strive
    to be honorable: they are exemplary.
Those who abandon righteousness and pursue evil
    we honor not at all, but revile.
But you, God Our Creator, in whom is no flaw,
    deserve our submission, obedience and worship.
You need none of these, for you need nothing,
    but we ourselves need to worship, to praise.
For without you we are nothing.
    So help us to worship you humbly.
We will not know the joy of life perfectly
    until we worship you perfectly, Our God.

61

When I peer into the night, God of Light,
still the moon rules the night.
And when the moon is hiding 'round the earth,
still the stars illuminate the sky.
But perilous and awful is that darkness
that lies outside your presence, God.
Once, I saw this darkness, and in my mind
I fell into it, descending with no end.
But my heart cried out to you, Savior,
who called out to me in the gospel,
And I was snatched up, cleansed and saved!
—saved from the final and utter darkness.
Oh, Merciful Lord, you own me. I am yours.
You may use me, guide me, send me,
And whatever time I have left in your plan,
I still yield it to you. Glorify yourself in me!

62

We are like you when we help each other, God.
From afar, even those who do not know you
Imitate you by some sense granted to us,
when you left with us your general grace.
Thus even in our sin you left enough of you
to keep us from rapid self-destruction.
But in your family, Loving Presence, you live,
and where you live, the help we give
Is not only to survive, but more, to bless,
to act out your love in us who believe.
I thank you, Divine Helper, for helpers here,
for selfless helpers who come to me in love.
Forgive me for years of mild ingratitude,
for expecting what none had to give.
Make me, at last, a helper, to the end,
and daily grateful for those who help me.

63

For your disciples, Perfect Teacher,
you gave a model for their prayers:
Your kingdom come, you said, they should ask,
the rule of God in all and over all.
Your time, O King, is no doubt set for coming;
our impatience cannot speed it.
But its negative image I pray for today,
within my own life and in those around me.
Less stubbornness, Master, and less pride,
less failure and less discouragement.
Less laziness in your will, less unconcern,
less wandering in attention to righteousness.
Less compromise with the trends of the world,
and less sorrow because of opportunity missed.
Your kingdom may come in the heavens after me.
but may it come in my life before I see you.

64

My God, in my youth I peered out to my future,
and I prayed for guidance, for your will.
You spoke to my heart and led me,
you gave me a calling, a task.
Along the way I prayed, Divine Leader,
for a course, when storms made me doubtful.
You pointed the way, you led me, you provided,
and I praised you for rescue and supply.
Amid a desolate time I sat bereft, as if lost,
and hoped for purpose yet in your will.
And in a moment of bright revelation
you guided me on again to do your will.
Now, I am in the shallows off heaven's shores,
and I seek some purpose yet in your plan.
Will you lead me yet, O Lord, that I, with Paul,
might finish my course, engaged in your will?

65

Eternal Word, you have said to us
we were created only a little lower than angels.
Yet we greatly sin if we vaunt ourselves
as something impressive, puffed up in pride.
You have told us, O God, that we are but dust,
and to dust we shall return.
Yet you have crowned us with honor,
and we have dignity for being made in your image.
Surely you have not planned that we
shall walk in confusion over our worth.
But we see that in the distortion caused by our sin
we shall not see your holiness aright,
Until we see our infinitesimal smallness
and our vast need of your grace upon us.
Daily bring my spirit to this humbling thought,
and I will worship you with all my being.

66

With holy envy today I think of him,
my brother in faith for whom I prayed,
Imploring you that you would relieve him,
carry him into your bosom into life of life.
You have stretched forth your merciful hand
and have taken him to his home.
I thank you, loving Savior, for this blessing,
though as nearly always the going was rough.
O that we had never sinned and made life hard!
—that we had never aspired to exceed ourselves!
As we lay this body to rest, Caring Father,
lay another soul upon my heart,
That I might pray each day for him or her,
and rejoice when in your will the answer comes.
And may some brother call my name today,
that by and by their prayers might be granted.

67

I sit in silent revery, meditating on you,
who are shrouded in holy mystery.
I stand in wondrous awe, searching for you,
who stand apart, though ever present.
I walk out from my prayer, to seek you,
who dwell in glorious light in heaven.
I sing a simple song of praise, of worship,
an utterance without words or tune.
I hear a growing chorus around me
joining me in my nameless song.
I see the angels appear beside me,
upholding my song and my praise,
Or, they lead me into purer praise—
they who have no sin and know you well.
O Praise the Lord! Sing his love, his power,
and his holiness, in the purity of this moment.

68

God of my infancy, I thank you!
  You nurtured me in protective love.
God of my childhood, I thank you!
  You led me by others, and I received you.
God of my youth, I thank you!
  You watched over me in dangerous years.
God of my grown years, I thank you!
  You gave me purpose and led me aright.
God of my family, I thank you!
  You brought all of us under your wing.
God of my senior days, I thank you!
  I have come into years of fulfilment.
God of my tomorrow, I thank you!
  I trust you to take me into greater faith.
God of my whole life, I thank you!
  Whatever betide, my life has been your gift!

69

Eternal Word, I have prayed you would speak,
yet just as true is that I must learn to listen.
I will listen to the silent oratory of creation,
for it holds volumes about your power.
I will listen for your voice in the stories of nations,
for so the prophets heard you loudly in them.
I will listen to you uttering truths through others,
in their pilgrimages and discoveries.
I will listen for your voice in the wisdom of the wise,
for what they cast out may catch me.
I will listen to the pregnant silences around me,
the victories or predicaments of fellow saints.
I will listen in the hidden recesses of my heart,
where the word hidden there may come alive.
And if I do not hear this hour or this day,
I will listen on, for you speak, in a still, small voice.

70

Jesus, Word Made Flesh, hear me now.
You were acquainted with our weakness.
Did you feel our frustrations—when you
marveled at people's lack of faith?
When you retreated from crowds to be alone?
When you sighed deeply and then healed?
I am tired in my soul this hour, Lord,
and I cannot explain why I languish.
My joy in you is secure, but my mind
is beset with unnamed worries and sorrows.
I cannot lift myself up; I need your hand.
I grieve for myself and others. I feel alone.
Your Spirit, Savior, is my only salvation
from this low estate and I welcome you.
Raise me up, O Christ, to feel your sunshine,
and to rejoice in the wonder of your love.

71

It troubles me, Holy Comforter, that oft
I cannot tune my inner self to speak to you.
At times I seem so dull of thought and feeling
that I cannot hear but divine rumblings,
I cannot speak but primal groanings,
to try to lift my soul heavenward.
Yet in those times I confess I am tired—
tired of heart, weary of body and of age.
I need your ministry to my harried heart;
I need both your soothing and energizing.
There is no reason today may not be joyful!
There is no cause that keeps me dull!
You have not called me to sadness or defeat,
but to rejoicing and to victory in Christ!
I rise in my heart; I lift up my hands;
I begin to worship, and you bless me!

72

Great Physician, kind and compassionate,
guide my physician with your omnipotent hand.
Lead him in his great curiosity to find truth.
Direct his search to uncover causes.
Show him the pathway of diseases,
and help him to help me, O Loving Lord.
In my youth you called to me, gave me a gift,
to help men see the truth of your word,
To guide seekers to the light, and
to show the rebellious their error.
You made me an earthly assistant to you,
in the ministry of the word to man.
And you have called man to heal diseases—
given them gifts to study and to discover.
Through my healer's hand, Great Physician,
heal this ailing body and bring me rejoicing!

73

How can they live, my Savior and God?
—they who do not know your salvation?
They who altogether deny you are,
lie to themselves and believe they are safe.
They who do not know if you are,
refuse to think deeply, hoping for the best.
They who know you are, but flee the truth,
hope against hope, hiding their eyes.
They who have a form of truth, but not its power,
comfort themselves in crafted deceit.
But how does anyone live, O my God,
and not know for certain heaven's gift?!
I could not go on this day or one more
without this certainty, that you have saved me.
O Sweet Redeemer, Jesus Christ, I love you,
for dying in my place, and living for my life!

74

When I contemplate your redeeming work,
O Savior, I cannot fathom it!
From all sides I marvel at it, for it is deep,
and mysterious, and incomprehensibly great.
How could you accept the death of the Son,
Great Father?—for what I alone have done?
You are not blind, God, like governments of men,
that care not who pays the fine for a guilty man.
Yet when a benefactor pays for a malefactor,
the debt is owed to him who paid—
And the debt of love I owe is all I am,
and beyond all that, to the end of time.
But how my sins were laid upon him who died,
the spotless Lamb of God, I cannot know.
And I shall spend eternity studying this act,
at the pierced feet of him who died for me.

75

You remind me by your Spirit, Lord,
  not to be of such obsession with the heavenly
That I should be of little earthly good,
  and so render myself of no service to you.
Now, however, understanding Savior,
  let me dwell on what I most long for in heaven.
I long for rest, the more my life is beset
  by that which denies my body rest from trouble.
I hope for peace, from the clattering of earth's rabble,
  the deafening noise of its entertainment.
I seek perfection, amidst the distortion
  of earthly things by sin and its perversion.
Most of all, Loving Triune God, I desire you,
  to be with and in you, secure and safe,
Without any want or hunger forever, and,
  without any cause ever again for tears.

76

Grant me a better day of prayer, Father,
than I endured, struggling to speak.
For what should have focused my concerns,
the discomforts that wanted urgencies,
Instead tempted me into discouragement,
and brought darkness into my day.
Testing became temptation, and I was weak;
distress overtook me, and I languished.
If not for your persistent patience with me,
I would have given in, but you held me up.
I stand now at the edge of the bright city,
your heavenly, holy dwelling, in prayer.
I look forward to knowing your presence there,
but until then I'll carry on, in your will.
Keep me uplifted in prayer, energized in action,
and surrendered to each moment's leading.

77

They have moved the landmarks, Divine Judge!
They have taken away the practices of elders.
They have become like the world around them,
as if to be like them were to build your kingdom.
Their praise is suspect, Lord of Glory!
It vibrates with the drums of your enemies.
Their words sound sincere, but they pretend:
they lie with their lives as they go about.
How shall the people displaced rise above it?
How will they persevere in the face of it?
They will seek your face in the conflict;
they will gather as one and stand fast.
Your Spirit will sustain them in Jesus Christ;
your grace will enable them to hold out.
For you know the dark hearts of the enemy,
and you know them whom you have called.

78

Who am I, Infinite God, in this vastness?
Who am I, Pervasive Presence, in the world?
Who am I to be heard on high when I pray
or to be regarded when I petition you, Almighty?
You have commanded me to pray, and yet,
do my requests resound at heaven's gates,
Or do they merit the angels' porting them
like censers of vital flame to your throne?
Perhaps the mass of your people in volume
unanimously sounding their petition,
Or storied saints whose works change the world,
would be heard and answered soon.
But I? Dear Lord, for what do my prayers count?
Will you hear me, Ever Prompting Spirit?
Grant that I may not count as nothing
what Jesus Christ died to save and anoint.

79

The ministering spirit who tends to me, Lord,
surely is aware of my smiles and tears;
He knows when I exult and when I struggle,
when I follow and when I stray.
What a great mystery is this delegation of yours,
this assignment of myriad tasks to them.
For you, Omnipotent God, can do all things
without servants, be they angel or man,
And yet, to your glory, you have created us all,
for a purpose complex and beyond understanding,
To fulfil our roles in your cosmic drama,
and to enjoy the results of your plan.
Therefore I will be confident that unseen servants
shall do your bidding, but it is you, O Lord—
On you alone I call for help and guidance,
for you alone are God, and my God, and my King.

80

If my worship arises in pressing times, God,
do you value it more for the trial I am in?
But then, if I worship you easily from pleasant life,
is my praise cheap or hollow to you?
Can I control whether my life is full of trouble,
or smooth and free of stress, O Sovereign?
But in this hour of vacillation from tedium
to tempest, from inspiration to emptiness,
I strain against a wall of spiritual resistance,
to find thoughts deep and words strong,
That I may worship you genuinely, full of joy,
that I may praise you quietly, from the heart.
I know that you accept my offering, Loving God,
because Christ entered the holy of holies.
So, imperfect as it is, God of Glory, receive it,
and sweep over me with your Spirit of Renewal.

81

In a rough country I traveled days,
    burning in heat, hungering in drought,
Exhausted in my wandering, searching for water,
    seeing no relief in the desert scape beyond.
But in the turn of a day you have come to me,
    you have blessed me with water and food.
You have turned the fiery skies into blue,
    and the perilous nights into rest.
Still, I hope for the kingdom, O King,
    when no turn of events will darken life.
I long for the final disappearance of evil
    into the darkness beyond your light,
Where the rebels have chosen to live forever,
    and where no taint of them shall touch us.
Praise you, King of the Eternal Kingdom, praise!
    My love and worship will grow until I see you!

82

You have given me no great burdens for prayer.
    Lord, my daily load is small and light:
My friends, Master, who also labor under illness,
    are eager for answers to their fervent requests,
And I join them, hoping for your gracious acts.
    And they covenant with me for the same;
These other wandering persons, God,
    I daily pray you will save, for my sake
And for the sake of their loved ones,
    who hope to see them in heaven's safety;
My family I lift to you, for guidance and faith
    in these end times—surely they are the end.
And those are all my burdens of prayer.
    And they are greater than I know.
So daily I will pick them up and lay before you
    the precious lives and souls of these my charges.

83

We pray, and in our requests often fail,
  and why? Because you care not?
Beyond debate, you care for each of us:
  you have shown us, in the sacrifices.
The first sin, covered with skins and blood,
  the sins of the chosen family with ram's blood,
And the continuing needs of your people—
  you provided for them through much trouble.
In time, you showed your loving care in Jesus,
  who answered every prayer with his death.
Is it not, instead, that our paltry prayers
  match not the pressing pursuits of God?
And how can the finite think to guide the infinite?
  or the ignorant instruct the omniscient?
So teach me to pray to see your answers first,
  and then to ask for what you have granted.

84

Still I do not understand, Loving Presence,
for all the hints in your expansive word.
I know that we must struggle—I see it,
in your saints' lives through the centuries.
It only makes sense, seeing that we all sin,
and we all share in the curse of it.
If every saint were suddenly freed from hurt,
freed from trouble, and the world saw it,
Would not every sinner rush upon the church
and throw himself upon your mercy?
But where would be the need of faith?
And would such belief be faith at all?
And me—where is my faith, O God?
—in my struggle how do I differ from the lost?
Unless I touch your face, My King, with my faith,
and that will bring me through at last.

85

I make music in my mind, Creator of All,
a melody of whatever is welling up inside.
In this moment it is calm, deliberate thanks,
as I am relieved to be relieved of bodily woes.
I confess that sometimes—ere long—it may be
respectful complaint, with minor notes beset.
Tomorrow, perhaps, the song will ascend in power,
carrying a tune of worship to your ears,
Or an urgent phrase of intercession, a plea,
placed upon my heart by you, yourself, to sing.
The symphony of psalms you inspire, my Lord,
is new every season of my life.
Sometimes sad, often plaintive, then exultant,
but you, Divine Composer, hear it willingly.
Play, then, my heart strings to your delight, and
bless me with the melody, in my deepest soul.

86

You, Eternal Father, loved your Earthly Son,
just as in eternity you are united in essence.
And that wonder of incarnation showed us
the perfect love that binds the Three in One.
Long ago you said, Let us create man in our image,
and as you did, you reflected yourself.
And in the beauty of your creation you told man
his children would be a heritage to him.
Man is blessed with a quiver full of children,
if they are sharp and true.
So on this day I lift my heart in thanks
for my quiver, whose number is small,
But whose strength is sure and flight is straight,
and who honor their father from their spirit.
In turn may they see sons and daughters
who like the Perfect Son please them wholly.

87

As we forgive those who sin against us—
so Jesus taught us to pray.
Redeemer, if I have withheld forgiveness from any,
in your tenderness bring my fault to mind,
And whether private prayer or personal touch
requires, I vow I will clear the debt.
Savior, if I have withheld confession from any,
in your convicting Spirit take hold of me,
And as the circle of transgression may require,
I will make a clean breast that I may be pure.
Yours and yours alone is the obedience of others;
I cannot make any heart forgive or confess.
Where men may owe me contrition or release,
you alone, Holy Spirit, can change their hearts.
But mine I submit to your daily work, that
I may be without regret or rebuke before you.

88

What longing possesses my heart, dear Lord,
to know what some long before have known—
In the mists of ancient history when you appeared,
disclosing yourself and the world beyond.
What yearning comes over me time to time,
to hear a voice from your realm, O Spirit,
Infused in my trembling, earthly, mortal mind,
revealing mysteries that lie beyond the visible.
I know, as the first men did, that glory exists.
I sense that just beyond this world I see,
Just an instant in time past my final breath,
lies a truer, perfect realm where I will see.
But I, like all left here in the wake of our sin,
must see by faith until heaven is opened.
It is hard. But on the report of better men than I,
I will believe, and soon I will touch you for real.

89

Great things for you, Lord of Life, great things
—the dream of many a beginning pilgrim.
Our thankfulness for salvation's precious gift
inspires our hearts to reach high and aim far.
We advance those dreams with confident plans
and count our strengths as assets to achieve.
And should the mystery of your will, Lord,
grant us strength to stay and time to last,
Perhaps our goals come near, and we succeed.
But most men dream on empty footings;
Most men build with unfounded assumptions;
and time and age and infirmity take their toll.
I have few dreams left for this world, my Jesus,
save to walk with you the rest of the way,
To know you in your resurrection power,
and finally to walk the vale and enter the light.

90

You call me to prayer and praise, Living Lord.
Sometimes in the deep of night I wake;
An uncertain song wanders through my mind
and I strain to hear it, but I pray, and then sleep.
As morning gilds the skies I may rise in praise,
quietly joyful for the sign of your presence.
In the day you may move and I may pray,
Draw me nearer, and angels supply the chords.
The gifts of gifted souls gone by are embedded
in my mind as jewels of the prayers of saints.
Till now the day is over, and your gentle Spirit
enfolds me in tender care and gives me peace.
And if you prod me more to open my eyes
that I might see glimpses of truth,
I have your blessing as I tell my love to you
then rest, in the joy of a single hour with you.

91

Holy King, what is my role in your kingdom?
    If any role but just to receive your goodness,
What service do you want of me, what work—
    that even now I may fulfill my part in your great plan?
Since you brought me into this creation, O God,
    I have filled some role for you:
A learner, a student of your truths, with a mind
    fresh from nothingness and eager to become;
A young disciple, the blank slate of parents,
    reflecting their devoted instruction in truth;
A man called to proclaim, training well, working,
    going forth to spread your kingdom message.
But in these latter years, beset by all that has
    befallen me, what role is left in your plan?
I softly plead this day you will disclose some task and
    fill me with your Spirit to do it well and finish strong.

92

Please lead me not, Loving God, into trial so hard
that I cannot endure! For I have little strength.
I have not faced what now I seem to face,
and my body cries to my soul for help.
I have exhausted my reserves, Strong Deity,
and I must have your Spirit poured out.
I must endure! —for myself if not for others.
For I would not fail myself in this hour—
Though I mean not to boast that I can endure
in my own strength, but in yours, my God.
Where is that infusion of your power? Where?
I crave it as a starving man craves food.
I turn heavenward in my heart and plead:
Spirit of Power, look with compassion into me,
Pour yourself into me, every crevice and cavern,
and enable me to endure my trial!

93

Worship in times of health and success is free
    and praise falls from our lips with ease.
Our joy, Glorious God, is easily spoken,
    and there lies no hint of stress in it.
Yet we followers of Christ—who suffered much,
    yet for the joy set before him endured the cross—
Are taught to count our trials joy, for the faith
    and perseverance they bring when endured.
Shall our worship be more constrained for this?
    Or shall our praise be less free because of pain?
When the curse of sin is lifted at last and gone,
    still our worship will be pure and free,
But while we suffer here, there's glory in our
    willed worship where many might withhold it.
So, from trembling hands and weary body I exult:
    you are my God, my King, my Eternal Everything!

94

Like many epochs before ours, Eternal Ruler,
these are days of striving in the world.
In the quietness of my secret place with you
I know the rumblings of the outside world go on.
Yet you taught me to pray for your kingdom, and
this truth stands, that yours is the kingdom, Lord,
Yours is the power, and yours is the glory forever;
what then does that leave for any other?
Men strive for their kingdoms, some building,
some stealing, all guarding and protecting.
Mortals vaunt their power over others,
to keep, to take, to conquer for their claims.
And sinners seek their own glory in the world,
for fame, for coerced honor, for profit.
But now in truth and in the end without contest,
No kingdom, power or glory will remain but yours.

95

You grind away at my life, Master Builder.
    You plow into my being to remove dross.
You reform and reshape me in these hours,
    amid days of stress and difficulty.
Did you not lay the axe to my woods
    when I was younger, or did I resist you?
Was discipline then an easier thing to bear,
    or did I not need then what now I require?
And if some purpose in it lies now,
    will you reveal it soon, that I may hope?
Or is it simply fitting me for the kingdom,
    where no redress remains, and joy abounds?
O God, I long to be your instrument of good,
    of gospel and godliness and of grace.
Then grind away at my earthliness! —
    I will gladly receive it, if blessing follows.

96

Encouragement. I seek it in this hour, my God,
  my Comforter—I seek it like life's gold.
My heart is low, my vision of daily dreams—
  it is a dim valley, needing sunshine to guide me.
Reassurance. I need it for any hope of living,
  my Rock—not because of active doubt,
But because of the weakness I, like us all,
  am vulnerable to while the adversary still prowls.
Reinforcement. I call it up from your Spirit,
  Captain of the Host, to face the enemy.
For all his personae, all its forms, make their
  last attacks at my flanks and hope to defeat me.
What troops can you spare me in this hour, God?
  What aid can you send this hour, within your will,
That I may endure another hour, so as to conquer,
  in this last phase of the campaign for your glory?

97

Lord God, in these years of closure,
    and also discovery and renewed joy,
Save me from insignificance in my living;
    no attention do I seek, but only to matter.
Save me from uselessness in my days of rest.
    No great work do I do, but to be busy I pray.
Save me from foolishness, which plagues the old.
    No folly do I contemplate, but guard my mind.
Save me from obscurity in my small world.
    No idol would I be, but let not wisdom be wasted.
Save me from idleness in my days of age.
    No famed quest may be mine, but some task give.
Save me from stubbornness in growing in you.
    No apostle may I be, but may I be all you want.
I am yours to command, O King, yours to lead.
    I still hear your call and I still follow your voice.

98

How do you suffer the millennia of false worship?
    Sovereign Lord, how can you let them curse you?
Of old those vile idol worshipers provoked you,
    and your anger toward them satisfies me.
In lands far away the ignorant devised superstitions,
    harming not each other, but lost just the same.
But worst, this great imposter who would curse your
    ancient people and the followers of your Christ.
He united a people around a lie that denied your word,
    and vowed to destroy all who did not submit.
How can you tolerate them long? And I—should I
    work for their salvation or pray for their judgment?
For you, Eternal God, a thousand years are as a day;
    you can wait, but I am mortal and impatient.
Just Lord, show me where to cast my pearls,
    and when to wait in silence for your judgment.

99

Divine Spirit, in and around me always,
come to me in my living this day and this do:
Give me the thoughts I should think,
rapturous or practical, caught up in your mind.
Generate in me the feelings I should feel,
for others, for the righteous, for the lost.
Develop the concern that should weigh on me,
the things that drive my prayer and action.
Lay upon me the burdens I should bear,
a share of others' or a secret concern.
Think in me the ideas I can ponder and enact,
that I might be productive in your kingdom.
Set before my mind and soul the goals of God,
that I might aim my life always to your will.
God of Grace, impart to me that grace for these,
that I might be pleasing to you this bright day.

100

To you my God, who brought me into being
in a land of liberty to worship, I worship you.
To you, Heavenly Father, who gave me to parents
who loved you, I proclaim my love of you.
To you, Divine Providence, who saw to my salvation,
I render the deepest thanks of a saved soul.
To you, Guiding God, who oversaw my growth,
I submit my discipled life with deepest thanks.
To you, Sending Spirit, who calls men to serve,
I offer my abiding thanks for the privilege to preach.
To you, Father, Son and Spirit in heaven,
I thank you for my family, united in faith.
To you, Timeless Creator, who has given me years,
I give my song of praise for length of days.
Praise God, from whom all these blessings have flowed!
I worship you now, and shall forever in your presence!

101

My words elude me, God of all knowledge.
  I open my mouth but I cannot say them.
Somewhere in my deepest deeps I have a thought,
  and it rises to my throat but halts on my tongue.
I cannot find the language. I feel it, but I am dumb,
  for I know that my best words are weak.
My choicest phrases are insufficient.
  How can a dust speck comprehend a planet, a sun?
How can it understand a universe of suns and galaxies,
  when you have not made me to comprehend you?
You have made me only to fellowship with you;
  I need not your magnitude to experience you.
I need not your intelligence to speak to you,
  nor your knowledge to know you.
Nor do I need your wisdom to learn from you;
  I need only to be with you, and you will be with me.

102

I sing hymns today to you, My Maker!
    I wake in the night with their words.
I cannot explain to myself where they come from,
    what need or prayer or impulse recalls them.
At last, I simply sing them,
    hoping they come to rest where needed.
The word comes to my mind, Word of God,
    and I do not always know why.
You direct me thereby, or it haunts me,
    and I pray it back to you,
Hoping for an answer—to what, I know not—
    but confident in my experience of you, that
If you spoke your word to me it was for a perfect reason,
    and I trust you for a perfect answer.
Let your song fill my heart and your word, too,
    that I might know what you are saying to me.

103

What can I give you, Master Giver?
How do I possibly give a worthy gift?
I have searched for some thing, some ability,
some resource, some extreme measure to give.
I cannot find it, this thing that could suffice,
that would even be a shadow of a shade worthy.
You have given of yourself in creation,
making worlds upon worlds in vast space,
And to us you have given a world of beauty,
and lives to live in this beauty and to enjoy.
Though we fell from the perfection you designed,
still, if we open our eyes we see your gifts,
And something rises in us, urging us to give,
to render to you something in return.
What can it be? It is all yours. But I will give
as much as I can know, my life, my all.

104

What a fool I would be, Omniscient God,
if I were to think that, with enough years,
I could think divine thoughts, know mysteries,
understand what lies beyond my mind now.
And yet, this has been the faulty quest of man
since he believed the lie of the deceiver:
"You shall be like God," he said, and man fell.
And we have fallen for this lie ever since.
For we have believed that with enough time
all divine mysteries would be revealed.
But dear Lord, it is not time we lack,
but capacity; for we cannot discover
What we have no capacity to take in,
no ability to learn; for we are man, not God.
So teach me, this day to be content with humanity,
and to worship you as God, as alone you are.

105

How sweet is the respite from dark days,
O God of Healing and Relief.
How delicious and treasured are moments of ease
in the midst of stress and trouble!
If your hand of providence had not granted it
there would have been no relief,
Despite the help of others, the medicines of man,
or the natural abatement of trial.
And you have granted me the companionship
of one who transmits your love and care.
For these blessings, Giver of All Good Gifts,
I give you thanks this day, and always.
Grant, O Knower of Men's Minds,
that I should remember your providence,
And that in the time of trouble I should say,
Thank you, Thank you, My Loving Lord.

106

It was not meant to be, O Spirit Divine,
that we should merely guess at your existence,
Groping in the darkness for some proof of you,
some saying the idea of you is fantasy.
We were not meant to be isolated from your presence,
no clue of you self-evident in this world.
And indeed, we are not without signs of you,
but we do not hear you daily or see your form.
Once, man walked with you in the garden,
heard your voice, and communed with you.
Our trial since his fall has been to see you
only in some harder way, by faith.
For while seeing is believing to those who doubt,
believing is seeing to those who seek.
And I, this day, am one who daily seeks,
and one day I shall see and know you in your glory.

107

When will we leave this violent world behind?
O Just Judge, when will its villainy be punished?
The evil minds of rebellious people devise perversion.
They scoff at the upright—more, they condemn them.
They attempt to lead nations into evil disguised,
as if perversion of your creation were advancement.
They promulgate lies to enhance their power—
indeed, they believe their own lies as well as others.
They twist your truths to support their preachments;
they pretend to do God's work while denying you.
When will we escape their vile leadership?
When will your kingdom come in full?
Lord God! Mighty King! Just Judge! Act!
For we who follow your Christ are beaten down.
Even when we rejoice in victorious skirmishes,
we long for the war to be over and the King to reign!

108

Who am I, Eternal Presence, in the ages of man?
I am hardly a speck in my own ancestry.
Solomon looked backward and peered forward
and he realized with sober heart that we disappear.
We go the way of all the earth and then are no more—
here. For we cross into your presence forever.
But how will we be remembered by those who follow?
For our own ancestries show names—
They are almost all of them names with little else,
dates they were born, dates they died, and what more?
And though a few history may know for good or ill,
the vast number of them were stepping stones,
Flesh and blood stepping stones to us, who are the same,
and those who come after us will know the same.
If I may not be remembered for any great good,
may my steps lead my descendants to you, my God!

109

I did not pray to chance, Most High God;
    I did not ask chance to favor me.
I did not pray to fate, O Divine Providence;
    I did not ask to be smiled upon by luck.
I did not pray to happenstance, O King of All;
    I did not ask for its random blessing.
I did not pray to an imagined deity, Lord God;
    I did not risk my words on a fantasy.
I prayed to you, Creator, Sustainer and King;
    I asked of you this needful thing.
I claimed your promises, sought to meet your conditions,
    endeavored in every way to obey so as to succeed.
And in one brief respite I rejoiced in an answer,
    but it disappeared like a morning mist.
How do I endure my discouragement, My Comforter?
    Where do I lodge my disappointment?

110

You Planner of Men's Lives, my God Above,
to you it all makes sense—this universe.
You know each life intricately and thoroughly;
no person's part in your infinite plan is obscure.
Yet I, with a hint of a mind in the dust of a body
cannot fathom my purpose from time to time.
I peer into the gloom of my uncertainties,
into the shrouded days ahead that are my future,
And I cannot understand my purpose now and then,
or what possible point there is in your leaving me.
Why do I suffer this, endure that, go through it all?
Whose life do I enrich or teach or help by mine?
I have asked these things again and again.
If you spoke, I have heard nothing.
I am weary of petitioning you, with no answer.
Perhaps it is because any answer would be beyond me.

111

What a blessing to have a friend,
O You who stick closer than a brother!
What a crutch for the sometimes crippled in spirit!
What a drink of water for one thirsty for answers!
I find myself humbled at the help of a friend,
and ashamed that I have not been his equal.
Teach me, Incarnate Teacher, from your example,
how to be a friend indeed.
Fill me when with others, to come alongside them—
not that I have all answers or can do everything.
But you can, Mighty Companion, and, perhaps,
through me you may touch this one or that.
I may never know—that will suffice.
But you know, and that, too, will suffice.
My Eternal Friend, use me to bless someone;
today may he be touched by Jesus through me.

112

O Compassionate Sovereign, touch me!
For the stealthy finger of disease has come.
It stroked me with its malevolence,
and it has laid me low again.
But touch me, and it will leave,
as Jesus touched the sick, and they became well.
I am left wondering what your purpose is;
I beg for some hint what design you have.
For now, while I am abed and very low,
in my deepest heart I will rise up and sing.
Glory to you, O Glorious God, for not abandoning us.
I praise you for your eternal plan!
For when these ills are no more,
and when this flesh has died,
Instantly I will be in your presence—
healed completely and forevermore!

113

Forgive me, O Divine Redeemer;
in your mercy continue to transfer his blood.
My Jesus, who embraced all humanity as a man,
gather me back close to you in fellowship.
Why are we weak? Why are we so vulnerable?
When tempted to breach our covenant—
However small it may seem—it leaves us in sorrow
till we turn back and gaze at the cross.
How long will we all—all of us disciples—
stay in this realm of weakness, stumbling?
I lean upon the everlasting arms, My Savior.
I open myself afresh to your working.
Let no words of mine reflect anything but good,
no thoughts depart from righteousness.
Let my love of you show in my love of others,
and your holiness seep to my bones.

114

Care for them who care for me, Loving God.
Reward them for their sacrifice of time.
Supply all their needs by your riches in glory.
They gave much; to them be much given.
I am blessed by them in these days,
and I have tried, though of little strength,
To bless them with my testimony of you:
in the place of great fear of life, I speak of Jesus.
Keep my witness strong, Lord of my life;
to those who know you not, may I seek opportunity.
To those who know you, may I find fellowship,
and return me to your service in health.
Touch me now, and day by day renew my strength.
Make me wise in my steps.
Make me ever grateful for others' presence,
as I am greatly grateful for yours, Abiding Spirit.

115

I must come into your holy presence, Lord;
I must approach your throne, O King.
I must have my sins forgiven, Blessed Redeemer;
I must have my emptiness filled, Holy Spirit.
I am without strength, Strong Deliverer,
and I know my strength comes from you.
I am full of uncertainty about days ahead,
and you alone, Eternal Word, know my future.
In my mind I stride toward you, angels helping;
the way has been paved by Jesus my Savior.
I imagine I see your throne, glorious with light;
I feel I know you are near, full of promise.
I reach out for hope, for wholeness, for love,
and you are all to me, in my hour of need.
Let me rest in your goodness, Gracious God,
and in the morning may I sing to you!

116

The wicked slay the righteous, O Mighty One;
they slay them to the applause of the evil!
The evil masquerade as good, slandering the right,
and they condemn the right!
When such violence is done, men of good hearts hope
that now repentance will sweep the land;
They hope that people may come together,
that bloodshed too far will provoke peace.
Shall it, Divine Peacemaker?
Or shall the enemy of man grow stronger?
Before the great Day of the Lord,
shall there be a time of unity?
Or shall the division grow utterly perilous,
with no peace in sight ever again?
O Coming King, command us in your army to
hold forth the banner of righteousness in the world.

117

All sufficient God, you need not our worship,
for you need nothing at all, nor ever have.
All Glorious King, you need not our praise,
nor even that of the creatures before you always.
But we, Wise God, need to worship you mightily,
for we are creatures owing you our all.
And we, Worthy Master, need to praise you always,
for we are, only because you are.
Therefore in my hours of struggle I worship you,
that I might know that you reign.
In my days of dark wonder I praise you,
that I might see through them in your light.
In my frequent pleas I desire healing,
but let me encounter you, and it will be well.
And now I rest in your sufficiency, Lord God,
and pray to see all other things dissolve in your light.

118

Help me to pray through my pain, Crucified One,
For you did, and without selfish complaint.
My woes are surely not near your suffering,
which in my holiest hours I cannot imagine.
Nor are my trials equal to the worst of others,
and my friends to comfort are many more.
Holy Spirit, sent to make Christ real to me,
I open my deepest heart and welcome your fulness.
I am at the end of myself, and if not,
bring me to that end, that I may want no more.
Glorious God, Timeless One, Ruler of Creation,
dwell richly in this small soul, now and always.
Overwhelm me in mercy; overshadow me in love;
use me to point others to you so they may know you.
I look into your glory; I see you enthroned;
I bow in worship; you are my Loving Savior.

119

Your glorious abode is in the fullest heavens,
their unfathomable expanse your grand habitation.
O Infinite God, each galaxy a brilliant room
in your palatial home, they light your creation.
We gaze on them, those whirling testimonies,
and we are pointed by a billion billion stars,,
We are directed to your infinite power;
we are shown the magnitude of your holiness.
Who but you could bring this into existence?
For nothingness begets nothing at all.
O ancient of Days, you have no past or future,
for you are in them both as in the present.
So we, as creatures who begin, inhabit time,
and we look to you to lead us to eternity.
I worship you, Father, Son and Spirit in One God;
I await the blessed hope as I stand before you.

120

This is the day you rose from the dead, Jesus—
Conquering Savior, Everlasting King!
This is the day you appeared first to your disciples,
showing them, as you have shown me, you are alive.
This is the day you appeared and Thomas believed,
and I am one who has not seen but has believed.
This is the day, O Glorious Redeemer,
that you went from earth to heaven.
And until your kingdom comes, you reign there,
while we pray daily you will appear soon, for us.
This is the day you sent your Spirit to us,
O Present and Holy God, inhabiting us.
And so we gather on this day, the Lord's Day,
to celebrate you as we join together.
So, let this be a day you make yourself known,
for we worship, love and thank you, Our Savior!

121

In the noiseless expanse of space
    the cacophony of earth may be lost,
The senseless sounds of human clatter,
    the empty chants of lost, frantic souls.
Into this deep, silent haven of reverie
    I soar, on wings of prayer this hour.
Let me find your palpable presence, Lord;
    envelop me in your quiet being.
I long to have no distance between us,
    to know no guesswork as to where you are.
I hunger for your voice to guide me,
    to reassure, to fulfill, to love me.
The disciples followed you, came to you,
    looked at you, heard you, spoke with you.
When will my faith be sight, O Glorious One,
    and these ragged clothes of flesh be new?

122

O Strong Deliverer, who bore my sins on the tree,
    bear me up in these hours of distress.
I do not suffer for the faith, my Master;
    I do not struggle with temptation—
Unless it is to believe less that you are near
    or that you will help me, or that you care.
But I do believe—for I am here, before you now,
    seeking your face for a ray of your sunshine.
Hold me up, for the feet of my faith falter—
    not simple faith I need, but trust with expectancy.
Said he who sought your healing, I do believe:
    help thou my unbelief; and you did.
So say I, Author and Finisher of Our Faith:
    calm every doubt and fear just now.
And in the bright morning of life's tomorrow
    I will remember no more these trials today.

123

How precious the gift that shall not be reclaimed;
how sweet the possession that cannot be lost!
O God of Promises, your offer received is life, and
you, Giver of Every Perfect Gift, do not repent.
How firm, then, the foundation for my life,
how solid the rock on which to build!
As one by one the earthly gifts of younger years
desert the body they graced with strength,
The fastness of your eternal life contrasts,
its permanence a growing joy, sustaining me.
O Saving Son, let me hold forth life to others
and make the joy of its reality plain to all.
Hone my skills to tell them what truly matters
and to point them to the way of salvation.
And those I name before you each day, save,
with the same eternal gift that gives me hope.

124

How, Divine Savior, how did you stay there—
stay on that cross all the way to death?
We shrink from pain, wince and pull back;
we writhe and then struggle to free ourselves.
How did you stay, O Incomprehensibly Great God?
How did you not escape, when you could?
For if legions of angels were at the ready,
and at your summons would have freed you,
I know you could have ended the pain,
halted your suffering, and said, No more.
But your purpose, steeled by Holy Spirit power,
your inner strength, undiminished by sin,
Your love, undeterred by physical pain,
kept you on the cross until your work was done.
And I, will I stay the course, though rarely hard,
or faint, when you were faithful to the last?

125

The nagging weakness of age, O Ageless Lord,
has made me feel the simpleton:
I stare into the wall, wondering nothing;
I drift into thoughtless sleep, distressed.
Any grandiose dreams I might have entertained
have dissipated into the humdrum of my world.
How will you use this thinning shell of a man?
What purpose can I serve, sitting uselessly?
My soul drifts out into the limitless sky
and envisions the hosts of heaven there,
Assembled in the gleaming brightness,
both emanating their holy worship
And absorbing the gracious effusions
of your loving and powerful presence.
O God, I, too, worship you, and long to be blessed;
forget not your least servant, as I wait for you.

126

Not for eternity in heaven did you ordain us,
O God of Perfect Love, to be one with our mates;
For like the angels we shall be, you said,
each one before you equally, in new robes of being.
But here, you have blessed us with the gift,
the mysterious gift of unity with another.
And I have thrilled to that gift these many years,
and how it sustains me in these days.
And now one dear to us joins hands and hearts
with another, their lives to join.
So before you I hold them up, awaiting blessing,
that what you, my Triune God, unite will endure.
Walk with them in the garden of their love,
and commune with them as they walk with you.
And by them may their world also be blessed
for having their testimony walking among it.

127

O God, in whom I believe, faith is hard;
 it is simple to choose, but difficult to do.
If, as your word says, faith is confidence in our hope,
 then it is sometimes fraught with failures.
And if it is assurance of the unseen,
 it struggles against the delay of your answers.
I do not doubt you, divine Keeper of Promises;
 I only fail to see you at work when I most need to.
My time is not your time, O Timeless God,
 my urgency not your priority.
Teach me the faith of the ancients, Lord,
 who grasped what they could not touch,
Who knew what they could not see,
 and struggled against what seemed disproof.
If they could suffer for forging on in faith, Lord,
 surely I can endure the day with your help.

128

I lift up my hands to offer praise to you, Lord;
    I bear in them feeble words, but earnest.
I open my hands to receive from you, Giving God;
    no man can give the blessing I so need.
I clasp my hands in prayer, O Mighty King;
    my fervent request is for your kingdom in my life.
I extend my hands toward you, Worthy God;
    what little I have and am, it is yours.
Today is all I have—and only this moment of it—
    to live surrendered to you fully, Master.
Step by step, light my way, for I do not know it;
    hour by hour, fill my heart, to make me bold.
More than ever in years gone by I need you now;
    more than when my vistas were wide.
For now, as the goal approaches, I aim for you,
    and I would not fail now to be faithful and true.

129

How the pursuits, the things, the cares of this earth,
pale when compared to what is to come, O Lord!
For though you will remake heaven and earth
and we shall live there one day,
There shall no taint of sin turn possessions to gods,
or tempt us in any way to misuse our freedom.
And as I see more clearly the darkness in this life,
the brightness of your eternal realm calls me.
I am each day more thrilled that you included me,
that you made a place in your heavenly house;
O Loving Redeemer, hasten the day when you come
to take us to be with you in a perfect world.
I long to see you face to face, no longer in my mind,
and until then I worship you within;
I have no worthy concept of your holy beauty:
but soon I will see you, and fall down in praise!

130

O Perfect Planner, your will for me is best.
  Yet you have said of the desires of my heart:
Delight yourself in me and they will be fulfilled;
  so I am privileged to pray for what I long for.
But ah, Wise God, you have not left to me,
  to my whim, what shall be my lot, my life.
For the kingdom is yours, and all of us yours,
  and our supreme prayer, Your will be done.
But it was there all the while, wasn't it!
  —in that couplet, for if I delight myself—
If I become absorbed in you, your great purposes,
  what can the desires of my heart be but yours?
O, teach me this science, this art, this passion,
  of taking every day's delight in who you are,
That finally when I pray, it will be for your will,
  and every answer from you will be Yes.

131

Father, Great God, Generous Provider,
I see my crust of bread this day,
And I thank you for it, for it is a gift,
my daily bread, my need met.
I see my presence here, in my simple abode,
with warmth enough and light enough,
And I thank you, for I could be in cold and dark
without a bed to lie on, or shelter from rain.
The day is dreary, but the flowers drink it in;
how like them I should be, thankful to you.
My trials make me wince in complaint,
until I remember they shall end, as this body will.
My woes darken my outlook, but then I say,
I can endure them in your strength.
For my hope is sure, and now my faith is stronger,
and with thanks I take another step toward you.

132

How many worlds are there, Powerful Creator,
where you have brought forth life, as here?
Any but ours, O Lord—where we have rebelled?
any but ours? and are they obedient and true?
For it seems arrogant of us to presume we are alone,
in a corner of your creative work, lost.
And I, I would presume much upon my worth
to imagine that you owe me any attention;
And yet I pray, believing you see me here,
that you know me, that you care for me.
And why? Because you have told me so,
in the truths of your acts handed down,
In the appearances of your Angel, and
in the coming of your Self in the Son.
So today, I presume only what you said do:
I bow my head and heart, and pray to you.

133

I come to you in fervent prayer, Lord,
and ask how long, how long until...
And softly back your Spirit says to me,
Trust me yet a little longer.
I do, and I shall trust you for life itself, my God,
without pause, forever in this world.
And yet, I pray, for this one thing how long?
and gently back your voice comes clearly,
Trust me yet a little longer;
in this thing, too, continue trusting.
Where else but you is there to go, O Lord,
for what I ask; where else could answer?
No power of man can give what now I ask,
and no mistake of chance can grant it.
So I will do what you have said, my God;
a little longer will I trust. Amen.

134

Your name, O Mighty and Majestic God,
is excellent in all the earth!
Though men do not exalt you everywhere,
and not all people honor you in every land,
The land itself honors you—formed as it was,
created in spilling colors and grand views,
The earth exalts you, as if it could speak,
and it does speak, as do the stars around us.
We hear them praise you with their voices of light;
we join their mighty chorus and sing Amen.
So my heart is lifted up this night to worship,
out of the darkness of daily tedium and trial.
I join the universe, the angels and saints alive,
and say, Glory to God in the Highest! Glory!
Let all my weary bones rest peacefully in prayer, till
with you, Savior, I begin to know eternity's bliss.

135

Agur of old said the leech has two daughters
who cry, Give, Give! and are never satisfied.
I would not be a selfish beggar, O My Lord,
who never comes before you with anything else,
Who always begs for more, without thanks and praise,
and who never worships without expectation.
But who, O Gracious God, can give what I need?
Who but you can fit me for life as well as death?
And have you not said to pray and not faint—
for even an unjust judge relents when pestered.
I come worshipfully, humbly, expectantly now,
and repeating my solemn, daily prayers,
For salvation for these, for healing for those,
for strength for others and for me.
Remember me, Jesus my Savior, and touch me now,
that I might rise up blessed, and tell others.

136

Searching Spirit, sometimes when I pray
I have been selfishly taken with my own needs, I have
Prayed less for others, who needed my intercession more.
Indeed, at times I demand of you answers,
When answers would not have satisfied,
or your purpose was beyond my comprehension.
Forgive my preoccupation with myself, Lord,
for I have let my trials tempt me to whine.
Surely my light distress is less than that of others,
and it is not meant to make me self-absorbed.
How, then, shall I leave this world of egotism
and be reoriented toward others, and you?
Show me the way, Loving Leader, Patient Guide;
show me how to follow you, Suffering Servant.
For if, when you were to be crucified, you washed
my feet, surely I am to serve others, even then.

137

Where is beauty in worship, Glorious King—
you who deserve excellence and pageantry?
How casually they present themselves before you,
without the beauty and grace of generations,
The mighty music of worship suddenly absent,
and failing to touch my soul or search my heart.
Abandoned, I turn to worship inside my soul,
to memories of the dignity of yesteryear.
Alive in my mind is the preaching with power then—
O Divine Word, where are your prophets today?
I must call them to mind and hear them in memory;
I read what they wrote; it reverberates in my soul.
But as I close on my end, I begin to hear heaven:
I feel its unsurpassable pageantry approaching.
I yearn for it and for your uninterrupted presence,
your fellowship with no separation, forever with me!

138

O Supreme Lawgiver, your first command:
to love you with my heart, soul, mind and strength.
And I do declare my love for you now and always.
But is avowing it enough? Surely not.
For Jesus said I was to love you by obedience.
And how? And what motivates me to do so?
Is it for creating me? For setting me down here,
so as my eyes open on the beauty of creation
I may so delight in it that I love you in thanks?
or in the discovery that you take fatherly care?
Or is it because your choose to include me in life,
and take me to glory someday soon—
For surely this is the greatest gift, and merits my love.
But beyond any gift I must love you alone;
For who you are, O Infinite One, I love you,
because you are my God, who first loved me.

139

Ever Present Spirit, be with me intensely
in these idle hours when I have no strength,
When health is failing and strength lagging
and I cannot go and do but must sit in need.
Never as in these hours would I yearn to act,
and I regret not acting when I could, as I could.
I have used this quietness to pray for others, Lord,
hopeful that your listening Spirit will answer.
Add to my burdens a care for others who need you,
to save, to heal, or to grow in Christlikeness.
But though I am pleased to be an intercessor,
still I implore you for health to rise and serve.
O Kind King, you who command your universe,
order my ills depart, that I may serve you—
and that, with new health—and schooled by its loss,
I may begin a new time of devotion in action.

140

Lord, my God, my life, my joy, my song,
	nothing from your hand this moment do I ask,
Except to know and feel your presence in my soul,
	for I need you, only you, more than any thing.
I have often sat in my place of daily prayer
	and have repeated my urgent requests—
And they are still urgent, O Divine Supplier;
	for they are unselfish intercessions for others.
And I have pled with you, Loving Father,
	for my health, that I might run with others,
That I might serve in strength, and go in energy.
	But this moment, this quiet moment of reflection,
I need only you, Holy and Wonderful Spirit,
	to make me whole and to set me at peace.
Fill me with your rich, beautiful fulness, Lord;
	raise me into the heavenly heights with you just now.

141

You have given me years to see my young wed,
O Wise Providence, and now they venture forth.
I am deeply aware of the world they face ahead,
and as tumultuous as my world was when young,
Their world is more frightening than ever, O God;
how could I have faced theirs with courage?
Surely, O King, your return is near—I feel it!
Do I not feel it, O Christ? Are you not coming?
For how can man's rebellion be more perverse—
and yet I know it could—but why do you wait?
But I must pray for them to be utterly faithful,
to stand for truth, to live purely, walk devoutly.
And their families, Father, keep them, keep them,
free from sin, safe from the world, sealed.
And if I depart before I see them grow fully,
let me leave assured you have granted this request.

142

O Divine Redeemer, forgive me for when I have
expended my energies in pursuit of little,
Where much lay in view that you offered instead,
or where paltry good was had instead of plenty.
Forgive my use of your resources on myself
when your use through me might have served you.
I know there have been frivolous ventures—
not just the enjoyment of life you bless—
But waste of your riches I might have spent on others,
that someone might have come to the kingdom.
I cannot undo my life—I am increasingly aware—
and time is not left equal to my neglect.
So this day, with the peace of your forgiveness,
give me a task at a time to make amends.
I commit to you each day forward to spend
the blessings you give on the missions you ordain.

143

Infinite Presence, I come to this place of prayer,
    where I worship, petition, struggle, question,
Where I hash out my guided wanderings,
    where I search to find wisdom and answers,
And I am dumb before you in this late hour;
    I cannot plumb a shallow thought.
I cannot fit this troubled mixture of events,
    the seemingly pointless happenings of these days,
Into a grand plan with only a glimpse for me,
    just a hint of why it is all happening.
Saying so makes me realize I am again
    confronting your inscrutable wisdom, Father.
Your infinite mind both devises and comprehends
    all plans for all men through all time.
I should not ask for more than this moment's notion,
    and for this I do, and I rest in you for the rest.

144

How precious my solitude, O Lord, my God.
How sweet the hours of silence, alone.
The psalmist communed with you on his bed,
his heart speaking noiselessly in this realm.
Not in sleep do I rest alone for communion;
my thoughts ascend in bright afternoons.
They rise to you in dreary mornings;
they query you and listen for you at midnight.
You prod me to consider the troubling thought;
you surprise me with little revelations.
Did the prophets of old hear you in loneliness?
Did they speak to you when no one was there?
Omnipresent Presence, you always hear me;
O that I would always hear you.
So in this hour alone, Divine Companion,
let me find you, and in the silence hear God.

145

O Holy and Righteous One, man is a sinner!
And out of that sin has come disease and death.
We labor under this weight, its inescapableness,
and we suffer until we are taken to you.
But even if we escape the worst ravages of disease,
we are prey to the ceaseless tempting of evil.
For what brought sickness brought more temptation,
the constant lure of what is desired but damning.
How thankful I am that age has brought me past
some destructive sins, and maturity past others.
Yet complacency remains, with its sinister laziness,
and discouragement, the bane of the ill and tired.
O Moving and Inspiring Spirit, save me
from these rotting wrongs, full of ruination.
Renew the spark in me each new day that keeps
me afire for you, ready both to live and share light.

146

Are there bells, O Praiseworthy King, in your realm?
Are there pipe organs, pianos, orchestras and drums?
Are there marching bands of angels in golden streets?
Do spontaneous crowds join in choruses of praise?
For surely you deserve constant worship, Holy God;
from deep within us and to the ends of creation.
Let the heavenly hosts with their voices and instruments
open up in a sforzando chord of celestial praise!
Let every redeemed soul awaiting resurrection shout:
To Our Great God Be Eternal Glory!
And through light years to galaxies we have yet to see,
may the high conductor's baton order ultimate praise!
Let every planet from billions of light years away be
heard in an instant, glorifying God who made them.
For Our God, The Only God, has been, is and shall be,
and we, his creation, owe him the highest praise!

147

Your word, Divine Revealer, catches me!
    It comes back to me in the day of my distress.
I pray and search, seeking you and your hand,
    and you are silent, and your hand is unfelt.
I beseech you, praise you, seek to worship you,
    plagued by the fear of some sin forgotten;
I find myself empty, peering into the dark,
    listening but not hearing, reaching, not feeling.
Discouragement sets in as I wonder
    if my energies are wasted, if you are not speaking.
And then I see your word in the book:
    Wait on the Lord. Wait on the Lord!
And one wrote there, Wait, and preached to me;
    and I soaked in the word and sat in reverie.
I shall wait on you, Lord, for your time to act;
    and I shall rejoice, for you have not forgotten me.

148

We are so small, O Great God of Glory.
    We are but specks upon whits upon dust.
And our planet, O King of All Creation, is small,
    and we can barely be seen upon it.
The greater and lesser lights are lost in the void,
    quickly left behind as the traveler goes out,
Into the galaxy and beyond, to see other worlds,
    and they, each one, are specks upon specks.
Why do we matter to you, Omniscient Creator?
    Why does our praise matter, our prayers, our lives?
Yet you have walked with us in the garden;
    you have chosen us to redeem, led us to your light.
I cannot discern the answers—I am but a speck.
    I am simply to seek you, find you as you find me;
I am but to walk with you, in you, and love you,
    and to render worship as befits every speck on earth.

149

O true Christians throughout the world,
faithful followers of Jesus the King, Rejoice!
For our King is robed and ready to return in glory,
to receive his everlasting Kingdom and to reign!
For his enemies, who fight his servants cruelly,
who deny the King, deny the word of God revealed,
Who set themselves against the spread of the gospel,
and who vow to suppress and then destroy it,
Are arrayed in vast numbers around the globe,
ready to march upon orders of their own king,
Whose hideous face they have not seen,
nor imagined it would be face of darkest evil.
And they, when they have amassed themselves
and united against you, Omnipotent Lord,
Shall unwittingly invoke your word: Lift up your heads!
For your final redemption is at the door!

150

God of Glory, Lord of All, Holy and Only God,
Creator of All that Is, Sustainer of Everything:
I come to you! I come out of a past of discovery;
I come out of a walk of struggle, and surviving.
I come, out of pilgrimage in the pathway of purpose;
I come out of plowed furrows of providence.
I come, through years of sharpening focus,
where each turn disciplined me to seek you.
I come, through harvest years of deep reward,
where you set before me a table of sufficiency.
I come! And I come with the loudest praise!
I come! And I come with the deepest worship!
I come through my heart and mind into your heavens,
and I shout your glory and sing of your goodness.
I come, because you are my God, now and evermore,
and you deserve my heart, my life, and my all!

www.ingramcontent.com/pod-product-compliance
Lightning Source LLC
Chambersburg PA
CBHW020357100426
42812CB00001B/101
9781737811763